SIMPLY
SOUP

LOVE
FOOD

This edition published in 2010

LOVE FOOD is an imprint of Parragon Books Ltd

Parragon
Queen Street House
4 Queen Street
Bath BA1 1HE, UK

ISBN 978-1-4075-9489-7

Printed in China

Cover design by Andrew Easton @ Ummagumma
Photography by Mike Cooper
Food styling by Carole Handslip and Sumi Glass
Introduction by Pamela Gwyther

Notes for the reader

• This book uses imperial, metric, and U.S. cup measurements. Follow the same units of measurement throughout; do not mix imperial and metric.
• All spoon measurements are level: teaspoons are assumed to be 5 ml, and tablespoons are assumed to be 15 ml.
• Unless otherwise stated, milk is assumed to be whole and eggs are medium. The times given are an approximate guide only.
• Some recipes contain nuts. If you are allergic to nuts, you should avoid using them and any products containing nuts.
• Recipes using raw or very lightly cooked eggs should be avoided by infants, the elderly, pregnant women, convalescents, and anyone suffering from illness.

CONTENTS

Introduction

If you cook nothing else, you could live exceptionally well on the rich variety of soups you will find in this easy-to-use book.

In many ways, soup is simple. It is either thin, as in consommé, or thick, either puréed or left chunky. This means that soups can be served in a variety of ways—thinner broths make perfect appetizers or healthy snacks, while more robust soups incorporating fish, meat, or vegetables can be meals in themselves. For even more diversity, some soups can even be served cold as well as hot—delicious on a hot summer's day.

There are many styles of soup using a huge variety of ingredients, with many countries having their own traditional favorites—dishes that are firmly entrenched in that nation's culinary history. To name just a few, think of Spanish Gazpacho and Greek Avgolemono, Italian Minestrone, and Ribollita, even Scottish Cullen Skink and Cock-a-leekie. Farther east there are spicy Middle Eastern recipes and Indian lentil-based dals. In the Far East, Thai flavors contrast with the blander Japanese Miso broth. Watch out for Bird's Nest Soup or Shark's Fin Soup when in China!

Soup making can be exciting and challenging, but don't be put off—all soups have three things in common, which makes them simple to understand and explore.

First, soup is very easy to make. Almost all soups start with sautéing an onion with a tasty vegetable, such as leek or celery, to build a flavor base. You simply add an appropriate stock, together with the main ingredients of your choice, and cook for long enough to soften the vegetables and bring out the flavors. It really couldn't be simpler!

Second, homemade soup is healthful. You can guarantee the quality of the raw ingredients, making sure that you are eating them in season and at the peak of their flavor. Usually there is very little fat involved and you can use the minimum amount of salt, which is why homemade soups are so much better for you than most commercially produced varieties.

Third, soup is so convenient. It is ideal—fresh, or quickly defrosted from the freezer—for a quick meal or impromptu dinner party at home, and it only needs a simple bowl for serving. It is easily portable too—just pack it into a thermos and you can enjoy a delicious cup of soup wherever and whenever you like.

Vegetable Stock

Makes about $8\frac{3}{4}$ cups

Ingredients

2 tbsp sunflower or corn oil
$\frac{1}{2}$ cup finely chopped onion
$\frac{1}{2}$ cup finely chopped leek
$\frac{2}{3}$ cup finely chopped carrots
4 celery stalks, finely chopped
$\frac{3}{4}$ cup finely chopped fennel
1 small tomato, finely chopped
10 cups water
1 bouquet garni

Heat the oil in a large pan. Add the onion and leek and cook over low heat, stirring occasionally, for 5 minutes, until softened. Add the remaining vegetables, cover, and cook for 10 minutes. Add the water and bouquet garni, bring to a boil, and simmer for 20 minutes.

Strain the stock into a bowl, let cool, cover, and store in the refrigerator. Use immediately or freeze in portions for up to 3 months.

Fish Stock

Makes about $5\frac{2}{3}$ cups

Ingredients

1 lb 7 oz/650 g white fish heads, bones, and trimmings, rinsed
1 onion, sliced
2 celery stalks, chopped
1 carrot, sliced
1 bay leaf
4 fresh parsley sprigs
4 black peppercorns
$\frac{1}{2}$ lemon, sliced
$5\frac{2}{3}$ cups water
$\frac{1}{2}$ cup dry white wine

Cut out and discard the gills from any fish heads, then place the heads, bones, and trimmings in a saucepan. Add all the remaining ingredients and gradually bring to a boil, skimming off the foam that rises to the surface. Partially cover and simmer for 25 minutes.

Strain the stock without pressing down on the contents of the sieve. Let cool, cover, and store in the refrigerator. Use immediately or freeze in portions for up to 3 months.

Chicken Stock

Makes about 11¼ cups

Ingredients

3 lb/1.3 kg chicken wings and necks
2 onions, cut into wedges
17½ cups water
2 carrots, coarsely chopped
2 celery stalks, coarsely chopped
10 fresh parsley sprigs
4 fresh thyme sprigs
2 bay leaves
10 black peppercorns

Put the chicken wings and necks and the onions in a large pan and cook over low heat, stirring frequently, until lightly browned.

Add the water and stir well to scrape off any sediment from the base of the pan. Gradually bring to a boil, skimming off the foam that rises to the surface. Add all the remaining ingredients, partially cover, and simmer for 3 hours.

Strain the stock into a bowl, let cool, cover, and store in the refrigerator. When cold, remove and discard the layer of fat from the surface. Use immediately or freeze in portions for up to 6 months.

Beef Stock

Makes about 7½ cups

Ingredients

2 lb 4 oz/1 kg beef marrow bones, cut into 3-inch/7.5-cm pieces
1 lb 7 oz/650 g braising beef in a single piece
12½ cups water
4 cloves
2 onions, halved
2 celery stalks, coarsely chopped
8 black peppercorns
1 bouquet garni

Place the bones in the base of a large pan and put the meat on top. Add the water and gradually bring to a boil, skimming off the foam that rises to the surface.

Press a clove into each onion half and add to the pan with the celery, peppercorns, and bouquet garni. Partially cover and simmer for 3 hours. Remove the meat and simmer for 1 hour more.

Strain the stock into a bowl, let cool, cover, and store in the refrigerator. When cold, remove and discard the layer of fat from the surface. Use immediately or freeze in portions for up to 6 months.

1

Classic Soups

In this chapter you will find all your old favorites, such as Tomato Soup and Chicken Noodle Soup, along with some more sophisticated combinations, including Clam & Corn Chowder and Bouillabaisse. There is nothing more welcoming than coming home to the aroma of freshly made soup, and these familiar favorites are sure to be a hit with the whole family.

Tomato Soup

SERVES 4

$^1/_4$ cup butter
1 small onion, finely chopped
1 lb/450 g tomatoes, coarsely chopped
1 bay leaf
3 tbsp all-purpose flour
$2^1/_2$ cups milk
salt and pepper
sprigs of fresh basil, to garnish

Melt half the butter in a pan. Add the onion and cook over low heat, stirring occasionally, for 5–6 minutes, until softened. Add the tomatoes and bay leaf and cook, stirring occasionally, for 15 minutes, or until pulpy.

Meanwhile, melt the remaining butter in another pan. Add the flour and cook, stirring constantly, for 1 minute. Remove the pan from the heat and gradually stir in the milk. Return to the heat, season with salt and pepper, and bring to a boil, stirring constantly. Continue to cook, stirring, until smooth and thickened.

When the tomatoes are pulpy, remove the pan from the heat. Discard the bay leaf and pour the tomato mixture into a food processor or blender. Process until smooth, then push through a fine strainer into a clean pan. Bring the tomato purée to a boil, then gradually stir it into the milk mixture. Season to taste with salt and pepper. Ladle into warmed bowls, garnish with basil, and serve immediately.

Minestrone

Heat the oil in a large pan. Add the garlic, onions, and prosciutto and cook over medium heat, stirring, for 3 minutes, until slightly softened. Add the red and orange bell peppers and the chopped tomatoes and cook for an additional 2 minutes, stirring. Stir in the stock, then add the celery, cranberry beans, cabbage, peas, and parsley. Season with salt and pepper. Bring to a boil, then lower the heat and simmer for 30 minutes.

Add the vermicelli to the pan. Cook for another 10–12 minutes, or according to the instructions on the package. Remove from the heat and ladle into serving bowls. Garnish with freshly grated Parmesan and serve immediately.

SERVES 4

2 tbsp olive oil
2 garlic cloves, chopped
2 red onions, chopped
2¾ oz/75 g prosciutto, sliced
1 red bell pepper, seeded and chopped
1 orange bell pepper, seeded and chopped
14 oz/400 g canned chopped tomatoes
4 cups vegetable stock
1 celery stalk, trimmed and sliced
14 oz/400 g canned cranberry beans, drained
3½ oz/100 g green leafy cabbage, shredded
2¾ oz/75 g frozen peas, thawed
1 tbsp chopped fresh parsley
2¾ oz/75 g dried vermicelli
salt and pepper
freshly grated Parmesan cheese, to garnish

French Onion Soup

SERVES 6

1 lb 8 oz/675 g onions

3 tbsp olive oil

4 garlic cloves, 3 chopped and 1 peeled and halved

1 tsp sugar

2 tsp chopped fresh thyme, plus extra sprigs to garnish

2 tbsp all-purpose flour

1/2 cup dry white wine

8 1/2 cups vegetable stock

6 slices French bread

10 1/2 oz/300 g Gruyère cheese, grated

Thinly slice the onions. Heat the oil in a large, heavy-bottom pan over medium-low heat, add the onions, and cook, stirring occasionally, for 10 minutes, or until they are just beginning to brown. Stir in the chopped garlic, sugar, and chopped thyme, then reduce the heat and cook, stirring occasionally, for 30 minutes, or until the onions are golden brown.

Sprinkle in the flour and cook, stirring constantly, for 1–2 minutes. Stir in the wine. Gradually stir in the stock and bring to a boil, skimming off any foam that rises to the surface, then reduce the heat and simmer for 45 minutes.

Meanwhile, preheat the broiler to medium. Toast the bread on both sides under the broiler, then rub the toast with the cut edges of the halved garlic clove.

Ladle the soup into 6 ovenproof bowls set on a baking sheet. Float a piece of toast in each bowl and divide the grated cheese among them. Place under the broiler for 2–3 minutes, or until the cheese has just melted. Garnish with thyme sprigs and serve immediately.

Spiced Pumpkin Soup

Heat the oil in a pan over medium heat. Add the onion and garlic and cook, stirring, for about 4 minutes, until slightly softened. Add the ginger, chile, cilantro, bay leaf, and pumpkin, and cook for another 3 minutes.

Pour in the stock and bring to a boil. Using a slotted spoon, skim any foam from the surface. Reduce the heat and simmer gently, stirring occasionally, for about 25 minutes, or until the pumpkin is tender. Remove from the heat, take out the bay leaf, and let cool a little.

Transfer the soup into a food processor or blender and process until smooth (you may have to do this in batches). Return the mixture to the rinsed-out pan and season to taste with salt and pepper. Reheat gently, stirring. Remove from the heat, pour into warmed soup bowls, garnish each one with a swirl of cream, and serve.

SERVES 4

2 tbsp olive oil
1 onion, chopped
1 garlic clove, chopped
1 tbsp chopped fresh ginger
1 small red chile, seeded and finely chopped
2 tbsp chopped fresh cilantro
1 bay leaf
2 lb 4 oz/1 kg pumpkin, peeled, seeded, and diced
2 1/2 cups vegetable stock
salt and pepper
light cream, to garnish

Split Pea & Ham Soup

Rinse the peas under cold running water. Put in a saucepan and cover generously with water. Bring to a boil and boil for 3 minutes, skimming off the foam from the surface. Drain the peas.

Heat the oil in a large saucepan over medium heat. Add the onion and cook for 3–4 minutes, stirring occasionally, until just softened.

Add the carrot and celery and continue cooking for 2 minutes. Add the peas, pour over the stock and water, and stir to combine.

Bring just to a boil and stir the ham into the soup. Add the thyme, marjoram, and bay leaf. Reduce the heat, cover, and cook gently for 1–1½ hours, until the ingredients are very soft. Remove the bay leaf.

Taste and adjust the seasoning, adding salt and pepper to taste. Ladle into warmed soup bowls and serve.

SERVES 6–8

1 lb 2 oz/500 g split green peas
1 tbsp olive oil
1 large onion, finely chopped
1 large carrot, finely chopped
1 celery stalk, finely chopped
4 cups chicken or vegetable stock
4 cups water
8 oz/225 g lean smoked ham, finely diced
¼ tsp dried thyme
¼ tsp dried marjoram
1 bay leaf
salt and pepper

Cream of Chicken Soup

Melt the butter in a large pan over medium heat. Add the shallots and cook, stirring, for 3 minutes, until slightly softened. Add the leek and cook for another 5 minutes, stirring. Add the chicken, stock, and herbs, and season with salt and pepper. Bring to a boil, then lower the heat and simmer for 25 minutes, until the chicken is tender and cooked through. Remove from the heat and let cool for 10 minutes.

Transfer the soup into a food processor or blender and process until smooth (you may need to do this in batches). Return the soup to the rinsed-out pan and warm over low heat for 5 minutes.

Stir in the cream and cook for another 2 minutes, then remove from the heat and ladle into serving bowls. Garnish with sprigs of thyme and serve immediately.

SERVES 4

3 tbsp butter
4 shallots, chopped
1 leek, sliced
1 lb/450 g skinless chicken breasts, chopped
2 1/2 cups chicken stock
1 tbsp chopped fresh parsley
1 tbsp chopped fresh thyme, plus extra sprigs to garnish
3/4 cup heavy cream
salt and pepper

Chicken Noodle Soup

SERVES 4–6

2 skinless chicken breasts
5 cups water or chicken stock
3 carrots, peeled and cut into 1/4-inch/5-mm slices
3 oz/85 g vermicelli (or other small noodles)
salt and pepper
fresh tarragon leaves, to garnish

Place the chicken breasts in a large saucepan, add the water, and bring to a simmer. Cook for 25–30 minutes. Skim any foam from the surface, if necessary. Remove the chicken from the stock and keep warm.

Continue to simmer the stock, add the carrots and vermicelli, and cook for 4–5 minutes.

Thinly slice or shred the chicken breasts and place in warmed serving dishes.

Season the soup to taste with salt and pepper and pour over the chicken. Serve immediately garnished with the tarragon.

Beef & Vegetable Soup

SERVES 4

1/3 cup pearl barley
5 cups beef stock
1 tsp dried mixed herbs
8 oz/225 g lean sirloin or porterhouse steak
1 large carrot, diced
1 leek, shredded
1 medium onion, chopped
2 celery stalks, sliced
salt and pepper
2 tbsp chopped fresh parsley, to garnish

Place the pearl barley in a large saucepan. Pour over the stock and add the mixed herbs. Bring to a boil, cover, and simmer gently over low heat for 10 minutes.

Meanwhile, trim any fat from the beef and cut the meat into thin strips.

Skim away any foam that has risen to the top of the stock with a flat ladle.

Add the beef, carrot, leek, onion, and celery to the pan. Bring back to a boil, cover, and simmer for about 1 hour or until the pearl barley, beef, and vegetables are just tender.

Skim away any remaining foam that has risen to the top of the soup with a flat ladle. Blot the surface with absorbent paper towels to remove any fat. Adjust the seasoning according to taste.

Ladle the soup into warmed bowls, garnish with chopped parsley, and serve hot.

Clam & Corn Chowder

SERVES 4

- 1 lb 10 oz/750 g clams, or 10 oz/280 g canned clams
- 2 tbsp dry white wine (if using fresh clams)
- 4 tsp butter
- 1 large onion, finely chopped
- 1 small carrot, finely diced
- 3 tbsp all-purpose flour
- 1 1/4 cups fish stock
- 3/4 cup water (if using canned clams)
- 1 lb/450 g potatoes, diced
- 1 cup corn kernels, thawed if frozen
- 2 cups whole milk
- salt and pepper
- chopped fresh parsley, to garnish

If using fresh clams, wash under cold running water. Discard any with broken shells or any that refuse to close when tapped. Put the clams into a heavy-bottom saucepan with the wine. Cover tightly, set over medium-high heat, and cook for 2–4 minutes, or until they open, shaking the pan occasionally. Discard any that remain closed. Remove the clams from the shells and strain the cooking liquid through a very fine mesh sieve; reserve both. If using canned clams, drain and rinse well.

Melt the butter in a large saucepan over medium-low heat. Add the onion and carrot and cook for 3–4 minutes, stirring frequently, until the onion is softened. Stir in the flour and continue cooking for 2 minutes.

Slowly add about half the stock and stir well, scraping the bottom of the pan to mix in the flour. Pour in the remaining stock and the reserved clam cooking liquid, or the water if using canned clams, and bring just to a boil, stirring.

Add the potatoes, corn, and milk and stir to combine. Reduce the heat and simmer gently, partially covered, for about 20 minutes, stirring occasionally, until all the vegetables are tender.

Chop the clams, if large. Stir in the clams and continue cooking for about 5 minutes, until heated through. Taste and adjust the seasoning, if needed.

Ladle the soup into bowls and sprinkle with parsley.

Bouillabaisse

Heat the oil in a large pan over medium heat. Add the garlic and onions and cook, stirring, for 3 minutes. Stir in the tomatoes, stock, wine, bay leaf, saffron, and herbs. Bring to a boil, reduce the heat, cover, and simmer for 30 minutes.

Meanwhile, soak the mussels in lightly salted water for 10 minutes. Scrub the shells under cold running water and pull off any beards. Discard any mussels with broken shells or any that refuse to close when tapped. Put the rest into a large pan with a little water, bring to a boil, and cook over high heat for 4 minutes. Remove from the heat and discard any that remain closed.

When the tomato mixture is cooked, rinse the fish, pat dry, and cut into chunks. Add to the pan and simmer for 5 minutes. Add the mussels, shrimp, and scallops, and season with salt and pepper to taste. Cook for 3 minutes, until the fish is cooked through. Remove from the heat, discard the bay leaf, and ladle into serving bowls.

SERVES 4

1/2 cup olive oil
3 garlic cloves, chopped
2 onions, chopped
2 tomatoes, seeded and chopped
2 3/4 cups fish stock
1 3/4 cups white wine
1 bay leaf
pinch of saffron threads
2 tbsp chopped fresh basil
2 tbsp chopped fresh parsley
7 oz/200 g live mussels
9 oz/250 g snapper or monkfish fillets
9 oz/250 g haddock fillets, skinned
7 oz/200 g shrimp, peeled and deveined
3 1/2 oz/100 g scallops
salt and pepper

2

Hearty Soups

These nourishing and satisfying bowlfuls are the ideal comfort food on a cold winter's day. Try Ribollita or Mushroom Barley Soup—both are meals in themselves, but if you are feeling particularly hungry, you can serve some chunks of fresh bread alongside. These soups will keep you going however hectic your day might be.

Roasted Mediterranean Vegetable Soup

SERVES 6

3 tbsp olive oil

1 lb 9 oz/700 g ripe tomatoes, skinned, cored, and halved

3 large yellow bell peppers, seeded and halved

3 zucchini, halved lengthwise

1 small eggplant, halved lengthwise

4 garlic cloves, halved

2 onions, cut into eighths

pinch of dried thyme

4 cups chicken, vegetable, or beef stock

1/2 cup light cream

salt and pepper

shredded basil leaves, to garnish

Preheat the oven to 375°F/190°C.

Brush a large shallow baking dish with olive oil. Laying them cut-side down, arrange the tomatoes, bell peppers, zucchini, and eggplant in one layer (use two dishes, if necessary). Tuck the garlic cloves and onion pieces into the gaps and drizzle the vegetables with the remaining olive oil. Season lightly with salt and pepper and sprinkle with the thyme.

Place in the preheated oven and bake, uncovered, for 30–35 minutes, or until soft and browned around the edges. Let cool, then scrape out the eggplant flesh and remove the skin from the bell peppers.

Working in batches, put the eggplant and bell pepper flesh, together with the tomatoes, zucchini, garlic, and onion, into a food processor and chop to the consistency of salsa; do not purée. Alternatively, place in a bowl and chop together with a knife.

Combine the stock and chopped vegetable mixture in a saucepan and simmer over medium heat for 20–30 minutes, until all the vegetables are tender and the flavors have completely blended.

Stir in the cream and simmer over low heat for about 5 minutes, stirring occasionally until hot. Taste and adjust the seasoning, if necessary. Ladle the soup into warmed bowls, garnish with basil, and serve.

Ribollita

Heat the oil in a large saucepan and cook the onions, carrots, and celery for 10–15 minutes, stirring frequently. Add the garlic, thyme, and salt and pepper to taste. Continue to cook for an additional 1–2 minutes, until the vegetables are golden and caramelized.

Add the cannellini beans to the pan and pour in the tomatoes. Add enough of the water to cover the vegetables. Bring to a boil and simmer for 20 minutes. Add the parsley and Tuscan kale and cook for an additional 5 minutes.

Stir in the bread and add a little more water, if needed. The soup should be thick.

Taste and adjust the seasoning, if needed. Ladle into warmed serving bowls and serve hot, drizzled with extra virgin olive oil.

SERVES 4

3 tbsp olive oil
2 medium red onions, coarsely chopped
3 carrots, sliced
3 celery stalks, coarsely chopped
3 garlic cloves, chopped
1 tbsp chopped fresh thyme
14 oz/400 g canned cannellini beans, drained and rinsed
14 oz/400 g canned chopped tomatoes
2$^{1}/_{2}$ cups water or vegetable stock
2 tbsp chopped fresh parsley
1 lb 2 oz/500 g Tuscan kale or Savoy cabbage, trimmed and sliced
1 small day-old ciabatta loaf, torn into small pieces
salt and pepper
extra virgin olive oil, to serve

Mushroom Barley Soup

Rinse the pearl barley and drain. Bring 2 cups of the stock to a boil in a small saucepan. Add the bay leaf and, if the stock is unsalted, add a large pinch of salt. Stir in the pearl barley, reduce the heat, cover, and simmer for 40 minutes.

Melt the butter in a large skillet over medium heat. Add the mushrooms and season with salt and pepper. Cook for about 8 minutes until they are golden brown, stirring occasionally at first, then more often after they start to color. Remove the mushrooms from the heat.

Heat the oil in a large saucepan over medium heat and add the onion and carrots. Cover and cook for about 3 minutes, stirring frequently, until the onion is softened.

Add the remaining stock and bring to a boil. Stir in the barley with its cooking liquid and add the mushrooms. Reduce the heat, cover, and simmer gently for about 20 minutes, or until the carrots are tender, stirring occasionally.

Stir in the tarragon and parsley. Taste and adjust the seasoning, if necessary. Ladle into warmed bowls, garnish with fresh parsley and tarragon, and serve.

SERVES 4

1/3 cup pearl barley
6 3/4 cups chicken or vegetable stock
1 bay leaf
1 tbsp butter
12 oz/350 g mushrooms, thinly sliced
1 tsp olive oil
1 onion, finely chopped
2 carrots, thinly sliced
1 tbsp chopped fresh tarragon, plus extra to garnish
1 tbsp chopped fresh parsley, plus extra to garnish
salt and pepper

Kidney Bean, Pumpkin & Tomato Soup

SERVES 4–6

- 9 oz/250 g dried kidney beans
- 1 tbsp olive oil
- 2 onions, finely chopped
- 4 garlic cloves, finely chopped
- 1 celery stalk, thinly sliced
- 1 carrot, halved and thinly sliced
- 5 cups water
- 2 tsp tomato paste
- 1/8 tsp dried thyme
- 1/8 tsp dried oregano
- 1/8 tsp ground cumin
- 1 bay leaf
- 14 oz/400 g canned chopped tomatoes
- 9 oz/250 g peeled pumpkin flesh, diced
- 1/4 tsp chili paste, or to taste
- salt and pepper
- fresh cilantro, to garnish

Pick over the beans, cover generously with cold water, and leave to soak for 6 hours or overnight. Drain the beans, put in a saucepan, and add enough cold water to cover by 2 inches. Bring to a boil and simmer for 10 minutes. Drain and rinse well.

Heat the oil in a large saucepan over medium heat. Add the onions, cover, and cook for 3–4 minutes, until they are just softened, stirring occasionally. Add the garlic, celery, and carrot, and continue cooking for 2 minutes.

Add the water, drained beans, tomato paste, thyme, oregano, cumin, and bay leaf. When the mixture begins to bubble, reduce the heat to low. Cover and simmer gently for 1 hour, stirring occasionally.

Stir in the tomatoes, pumpkin, and chili paste and continue simmering for an additional hour, or until the beans and pumpkin are tender, stirring from time to time.

Season to taste with salt and pepper and stir in a little more chili paste, if desired. Ladle the soup into bowls, garnish with cilantro, and serve.

Chicken Gumbo Soup

Heat the oil in a large, heavy-bottom saucepan over medium-low heat and stir in the flour. Cook for about 15 minutes, stirring occasionally, until the mixture is a rich golden brown.

Add the onion, green bell pepper, and celery and continue cooking for about 10 minutes, until the onion softens.

Slowly pour in the stock and bring to a boil, stirring well and scraping the bottom of the pan to mix in the flour. Remove the pan from the heat.

Add the tomatoes and garlic. Stir in the okra and rice and season to taste with salt and pepper. Reduce the heat, cover, and simmer for 20 minutes, or until the okra is tender.

Add the chicken and sausage and continue simmering for about 10 minutes. Taste and adjust the seasoning, if necessary, and ladle into warmed bowls to serve.

SERVES 6

2 tbsp olive oil
4 tbsp all-purpose flour
1 onion, finely chopped
1 small green bell pepper, seeded and finely chopped
1 celery stalk, finely chopped
5 cups chicken stock
14 oz/400 g canned chopped tomatoes
3 garlic cloves, finely chopped or crushed
4½ oz/125 g okra, stems removed, cut into ¼-inch/5-mm thick slices
4 tbsp white rice
7 oz/200 g cooked chicken, cubed
4 oz/115 g cooked garlic sausage, sliced or cubed
salt and pepper

Chicken & Potato Soup with Bacon

SERVES 4

- 1 tbsp butter
- 2 garlic cloves, chopped
- 1 onion, sliced
- 9 oz/250 g smoked lean bacon, chopped
- 2 large leeks, sliced
- 2 tbsp all-purpose flour
- 4 cups chicken stock
- 1 lb 12 oz/800 g potatoes, chopped
- 7 oz/200 g skinless chicken breast, chopped
- 4 tbsp heavy cream
- salt and pepper
- cooked bacon and sprigs of fresh flat-leaf parsley, to garnish

Melt the butter in a large pan over medium heat. Add the garlic and onion and cook, stirring, for 3 minutes, until slightly softened. Add the chopped bacon and leeks and cook for another 3 minutes, stirring.

In a bowl, mix the flour with enough stock to make a smooth paste and stir it into the pan. Cook, stirring, for 2 minutes. Pour in the remaining stock, then add the potatoes and chicken. Season with salt and pepper. Bring to a boil, then lower the heat and simmer for 25 minutes, until the chicken and potatoes are tender and cooked through.

Stir in the cream and cook for another 2 minutes, then remove from the heat and ladle into serving bowls. Garnish with the cooked bacon and flat-leaf parsley and serve immediately.

Sausage & Red Cabbage Soup

Heat the oil in a large pan. Add the garlic and onion and cook over medium heat, stirring, for 3 minutes, until slightly softened. Add the leek and cook for another 3 minutes, stirring.

In a bowl, mix the cornstarch with enough stock to make a smooth paste, then stir it into the pan. Cook, stirring, for 2 minutes. Stir in the remaining stock, then add the potatoes and sausages. Season with salt and pepper. Bring to a boil, then lower the heat and simmer for 25 minutes.

Add the red cabbage and black-eyed peas and cook for 10 minutes, then stir in the cream and cook for another 5 minutes. Remove from the heat and ladle into serving bowls. Garnish with ground paprika and serve immediately.

SERVES 4

2 tbsp olive oil
1 garlic clove, chopped
1 large onion, chopped
1 large leek, sliced
2 tbsp cornstarch
4 cups vegetable stock
1 lb/450 g potatoes, sliced
7 oz/200 g skinless sausages, sliced
5 1/2 oz/150 g red cabbage, chopped
7 oz/200 g canned black-eyed peas, drained
1/2 cup heavy cream
salt and pepper
ground paprika, to garnish

Hearty Winter Broth

Heat the vegetable oil in a large, heavy-bottom saucepan and add the pieces of lamb, turning them to seal and brown on both sides. Lift the lamb out of the pan and set aside until ready to use.

Add the onion, carrots, and leeks to the saucepan and cook gently for about 3 minutes.

Return the lamb to the saucepan and add the vegetable stock, bay leaf, parsley, and pearl barley to the saucepan. Bring the mixture in the pan to a boil, then reduce the heat. Cover and simmer for 1½–2 hours.

Discard the parsley sprigs. Lift the pieces of lamb from the broth and allow them to cool slightly. Remove the bones and any fat and chop the meat. Return the lamb to the broth and reheat gently. Season to taste with salt and pepper.

It is advisable to prepare this soup a day ahead, then let it cool, cover, and refrigerate overnight. When ready to serve, remove and discard the layer of fat from the surface and reheat the soup gently. Ladle into warmed bowls and serve immediately.

SERVES 4

1 tbsp vegetable oil

1 lb 2 oz/500 g lean neck of lamb

1 large onion, sliced

2 carrots, sliced

2 leeks, sliced

4 cups vegetable stock

1 bay leaf

sprigs of fresh parsley

2 oz/55 g pearl barley

salt and pepper

Beef & Bean Soup

Heat the oil in a large pan over medium heat. Add the onion and garlic and cook, stirring frequently, for 5 minutes, or until softened. Add the bell pepper and carrots and cook for an additional 5 minutes.

Meanwhile, drain the peas, reserving the liquid from the can. Place two-thirds of the peas, reserving the remainder, in a food processor or blender with the pea liquid and process until smooth.

Add the ground beef to the pan and cook, stirring constantly, to break up any lumps, until well browned. Add the spices and cook, stirring, for 2 minutes. Add the cabbage, tomatoes, stock, and puréed peas and season to taste with salt and pepper. Bring to a boil, then reduce the heat, cover, and let simmer for 15 minutes, or until the vegetables are tender.

Stir in the reserved peas, cover, and simmer for an additional 5 minutes. Ladle the soup into warmed soup bowls and serve.

SERVES 4

2 tbsp vegetable oil
1 large onion, finely chopped
2 garlic cloves, finely chopped
1 green bell pepper, seeded and sliced
2 carrots, sliced
14 oz/400 g canned black-eyed peas
1 cup fresh ground beef
1 tsp each ground cumin, chili powder, and paprika
1/4 head of cabbage, sliced
8 oz/225 g tomatoes, peeled and chopped
2 1/2 cups beef stock
salt and pepper

Seafood Chowder

SERVES 6

2 lb 4 oz/1 kg live mussels
4 tbsp all-purpose flour
$6^1/_4$ cups fish stock
1 tbsp butter
1 large onion, finely chopped
12 oz/350 g skinless whitefish fillets, such as cod, sole, or haddock
7 oz/200 g cooked or raw peeled shrimp
$1^1/_4$ cups heavy cream
salt and pepper
snipped fresh dill, to garnish

Discard any mussels with broken shells or any that refuse to close when tapped. Rinse, pull off any beards, and if there are barnacles, scrape them off with a knife under cold running water. Put the mussels in a large heavy-bottom saucepan. Cover tightly and cook over high heat for about 4 minutes, or until the mussels open, shaking the pan occasionally. Discard any that remain closed. When they are cool enough to handle, remove the mussels from the shells, adding any additional juices to the cooking liquid. Strain the cooking liquid through a cheesecloth-lined sieve and reserve.

Put the flour in a mixing bowl and very slowly whisk in enough of the stock to make a thick paste. Whisk in a little more stock to make a smooth liquid.

Melt the butter in heavy-bottom saucepan over medium-low heat. Add the onion, cover, and cook for about 5 minutes, stirring frequently, until it softens.

Add the remaining fish stock and bring to a boil. Slowly whisk in the flour mixture until well combined and bring back to a boil, whisking constantly. Add the mussel cooking liquid. Season with salt, if needed, and pepper. Reduce the heat and simmer, partially covered, for 15 minutes.

Add the fish and mussels and continue simmering, stirring occasionally, for about 5 minutes, or until the fish is cooked and begins to flake.

Stir in the shrimp and cream. Taste and adjust the seasoning. Simmer for a few minutes longer to heat through. Ladle into warmed bowls, sprinkle with dill, and serve.

3

Refreshing Soups

The recipes in this section are light in texture and fresh in taste, making them perfect for the summer months or as an elegant appetizer. Try Chilled Avocado Soup on a hot day, or Wonton Soup when it's a little cooler out. Remember that the fresher the ingredients, the fuller the flavor of the soup, so make sure you use fresh seasonal produce for the best results.

Vichyssoise

SERVES 6

- 3 large leeks
- 3 tbsp butter or margarine
- 1 onion, thinly sliced
- 1 lb/450 g potatoes, chopped
- 3 1/2 cups vegetable stock
- 2 tsp lemon juice
- pinch of ground nutmeg
- 1/4 tsp ground coriander
- 1 bay leaf
- 1 egg yolk
- 2/3 cup light cream
- salt and white pepper
- freshly snipped chives, to garnish

Trim the leeks and remove most of the green part. Slice the white part of the leeks very finely.

Melt the butter in a saucepan. Add the leeks and onion and cook, stirring occasionally, for about 5 minutes, without browning.

Add the potatoes, stock, lemon juice, nutmeg, coriander, and bay leaf to the pan, season to taste with salt and pepper, and bring to a boil. Cover and simmer for about 30 minutes, until all the vegetables are very soft.

Cool the soup a little, remove and discard the bay leaf, and then press through a strainer or process in a food processor or blender until smooth. Pour into a clean pan.

Blend the egg yolk into the cream, add a little of the soup to the mixture, and then whisk it all back into the soup and reheat gently, without boiling. Adjust the seasoning to taste. Cool and then chill thoroughly in the refrigerator.

Serve the soup sprinkled with freshly snipped chives.

Chilled Avocado Soup

SERVES 4

- 1 tbsp lemon juice
- 2 avocados
- 1 tbsp snipped fresh chives, plus extra to garnish
- 1 tbsp chopped fresh flat-leaf parsley
- 2 cups cold chicken stock
- 1 1/4 cups light cream, plus extra to garnish
- dash of Worcestershire sauce
- salt and pepper

Put the lemon juice into a food processor or blender. Halve the avocados and remove the pits. Scoop out the flesh and chop coarsely.

Place the avocado flesh, chives, parsley, stock, cream, and Worcestershire sauce in the food processor or blender and process to a smooth purée.

Transfer to a bowl and season to taste with salt and pepper. Cover the bowl tightly with plastic wrap and chill in the refrigerator for at least 30 minutes.

To serve, stir, then ladle into chilled soup bowls and garnish with a swirl of cream and a sprinkling of snipped chives.

Miso Soup

SERVES 4

4 cups water

2 tsp dashi granules

6 oz/175 g silken tofu, drained and cut into small cubes

4 shiitake mushrooms, finely sliced

4 tbsp miso paste

2 scallions, chopped

Put the water in a large pan with the dashi granules and bring to a boil. Add the tofu and mushrooms, reduce the heat, and simmer for 3 minutes.

Stir in the miso paste and simmer gently, stirring, until it has dissolved.

Add the scallions and serve immediately. If you leave the soup, the miso will settle, so give the soup a thorough stir before serving to recombine.

Gazpacho

SERVES 4

9 oz/250 g white bread slices, crusts removed

1 lb 9 oz/700 g tomatoes, peeled and chopped

3 garlic cloves, coarsely chopped

2 red bell peppers, seeded and chopped

1 cucumber, peeled, seeded, and chopped

5 tbsp extra virgin olive oil

5 tbsp red wine vinegar

1 tbsp tomato paste

9 1/2 cups water

salt and pepper

4 ice cubes, to serve

Tear the bread into pieces and place in a blender. Process briefly to make breadcrumbs and transfer to a large bowl. Add the tomatoes, garlic, bell peppers, cucumber, olive oil, vinegar, and tomato paste. Mix well.

Working in batches, place the tomato mixture with about the same amount of the measured water in the food processor or blender and process to a purée. Transfer to another bowl. When all the tomato mixture and water have been blended together, stir well and season to taste with salt and pepper. Cover with plastic wrap and chill in the refrigerator for at least 2 hours, but no longer than 12 hours.

When ready to serve, pour the soup into chilled serving bowls and float an ice cube in each bowl.

Chilled Borscht

Cover the cabbage generously with cold water in a pan. Bring to a boil, boil for 3 minutes, then drain.

Heat the oil in a large saucepan over medium-low heat. Add the onion and leek, cover, and cook for about 5 minutes, stirring occasionally, until the vegetables begin to soften.

Add the tomatoes, water, carrot, parsnip, beets, and bay leaf. Stir in the blanched cabbage and add a large pinch of salt. Bring to a boil, reduce the heat, and simmer for about 1¼ hours, until all the vegetables are tender. Remove and discard the bay leaf.

Allow the soup to cool slightly, then transfer to a food processor or blender and process until smooth, working in batches if necessary. (If using a food processor, strain off the cooking liquid and reserve. Purée the soup solids with enough cooking liquid to moisten them, then combine with the remaining liquid.)

Scrape the soup into a large container and stir in the tomato juice. Allow to cool and refrigerate until cold.

Add the dill and stir. Thin the soup with more tomato juice or water, if desired. Season to taste with salt and pepper and, if you prefer it less sweet, add a few drops of lemon juice. Ladle into chilled soup bowls and top each with a spoonful of sour cream and a sprig of dill.

SERVES 4–6

1/4 head of cabbage, cored and coarsely chopped
1 tbsp vegetable oil
1 onion, finely chopped
1 leek, halved lengthwise and sliced
14 oz/400 g canned peeled tomatoes
5 cups water, plus extra if needed
1 carrot, thinly sliced
1 small parsnip, finely chopped
3 beets (raw or cooked), peeled and cubed
1 bay leaf
1 1/2 cups tomato juice, plus extra if needed
2–3 tbsp chopped fresh dill, plus extra sprigs to garnish
fresh lemon juice (optional)
salt and pepper
sour cream or yogurt, to garnish

Lemon Veal Soup with Mushrooms

Put the veal in a large saucepan and add the stock. Bring just to a boil and skim off any foam that rises to the surface.

Add the onion, carrots, garlic, lemon rind, and bay leaf. Season with salt and pepper. Reduce the heat and simmer, partially covered, for about 45 minutes, stirring occasionally, until the veal is very tender.

Remove the veal and carrots with a slotted spoon and reserve, covered. Strain the stock into a clean saucepan. Discard the onion, garlic, lemon rind, and bay leaf.

Melt the butter in a skillet over medium-high heat. Add the mushrooms, season, and cook gently until lightly golden. Reserve with the veal and carrots.

Mix together the cornstarch and cream. Bring the cooking liquid just to a boil and whisk in the cream mixture. Boil very gently for 2–3 minutes, until it thickens, whisking almost constantly.

Add the reserved meat and vegetables to the soup and simmer over low heat for about 5 minutes, until heated through. Taste and adjust the seasoning, adding nutmeg and a squeeze of lemon juice, if using. Stir in the parsley, then ladle into warmed bowls and serve.

SERVES 4

12 oz/350 g boneless veal, cut into 1/2-inch/1-cm pieces
4 cups chicken stock
1 onion, quartered
2 carrots, thinly sliced
2 garlic cloves, halved
1 pared strip lemon rind
1 bay leaf
1 tbsp butter
12 oz/350 g small button mushrooms, quartered
4 tbsp cornstarch
1/2 cup heavy cream
freshly grated nutmeg
fresh lemon juice, to taste (optional)
1–2 tbsp chopped fresh parsley
salt and pepper

Wonton Soup

For the wonton filling, mix together the pork, shrimp, ginger, soy sauce, rice wine, scallion, sugar, pepper, and sesame oil, and stir well until the texture is thick and pasty. Set aside for at least 20 minutes.

To make the wontons, place a teaspoon of the filling at the center of a wrapper. Brush the edges with a little egg white. Bring the opposite points toward each other and press the edges together, creating a flowerlike shape. Repeat with the remaining wrappers and filling.

To make the soup, bring the stock to a boil and add the salt and pepper. Boil the wontons in the stock for about 5 minutes, or until the wrappers begin to wrinkle around the filling.

To serve, put the scallion in individual bowls, spoon in the wontons and soup, and sprinkle with the cilantro.

SERVES 6–8

8 cups chicken stock
2 tsp salt
1/2 tsp white pepper
2 tbsp finely chopped scallion
1 tbsp chopped cilantro leaves, to serve

wontons

6 oz/175 g ground pork, not too lean
8 oz/225 g raw shrimp, peeled, deveined, and chopped
1/2 tsp finely chopped fresh ginger
1 tbsp light soy sauce
1 tbsp Chinese rice wine
2 tsp finely chopped scallion
pinch of sugar
pinch of white pepper
dash of sesame oil
30 square wonton wrappers
1 egg white, lightly beaten

Consommé

Put the stock and ground beef in a saucepan and let stand for 1 hour. Add the tomatoes, carrots, onion, celery, turnip, if using, bouquet garni, 2 of the egg whites, the crushed shells of 2 of the eggs, and plenty of seasoning. Bring almost to the boiling point, whisking hard all the time with a flat whisk.

Cover and simmer for 1 hour, taking care not to allow the layer of froth on top of the soup to break.

Pour the soup through a colander lined with two layers of cheesecloth, keeping the froth back until the end, then pour the ingredients through the cloth again into a clean pan. The resulting liquid should be clear.

If the soup is not quite clear, return it to the pan with another egg white and the crushed shells of 2 more eggs. Repeat the whisking process as before and then boil for 10 minutes; strain again.

Add the sherry, if using, to the soup and reheat gently. Place the garnish in the warmed soup bowls and carefully pour in the soup. Serve immediately.

SERVES 4–6

5 cups beef stock
1 cup fresh extra-lean ground beef
2 tomatoes, skinned, seeded, and chopped
2 large carrots, chopped
1 large onion, chopped
2 celery stalks, chopped
1 turnip, chopped (optional)
1 bouquet garni
2–3 egg whites
shells of 2–4 eggs, crushed
1–2 tbsp sherry (optional)
salt and pepper
julienne strips of raw carrot, turnip, celery, or celeriac, to garnish

Seared Scallops in Garlic Broth

SERVES 4

- 1 large garlic bulb (about 3 1/2 oz/100 g), separated into unpeeled cloves
- 1 celery stalk, chopped
- 1 carrot, chopped
- 1 onion, chopped
- 10 peppercorns
- 5–6 parsley stems
- 5 cups water
- 8 oz/225 g large sea scallops
- 1 tbsp oil
- salt and pepper
- fresh cilantro leaves, to garnish

Combine the garlic cloves, celery, carrot, onion, peppercorns, parsley stems, and water in a saucepan with a good pinch of salt. Bring to a boil, reduce the heat, and simmer, partially covered, for 30–45 minutes.

Strain the stock into a clean saucepan. Taste and adjust the seasoning, and keep hot.

If using sea scallops, slice in half to form 2 thinner rounds from each. (If the scallops are very large, slice them into 3 rounds.) Sprinkle with salt and pepper.

Heat the oil in a skillet over medium-high heat and cook the scallops on one side for 1–2 minutes, until lightly browned and the flesh becomes opaque.

Divide the scallops among 4 warmed shallow bowls, arranging them browned-side up. Ladle the soup over the scallops, then float a few cilantro leaves on top. Serve immediately.

Cold Cucumber & Smoked Salmon Soup

SERVES 4

2 tsp oil
1 large onion, finely chopped
1 large cucumber, peeled, seeded, and sliced
1 small potato, diced
1 celery stalk, finely chopped
4 cups chicken or vegetable stock
$1^2/_3$ cups heavy cream
$5^1/_2$ oz/150 g smoked salmon, finely diced
2 tbsp snipped fresh chives
salt and pepper

Heat the oil in a large saucepan over medium heat. Add the onion and cook for about 3 minutes, until it begins to soften.

Add the cucumber, potato, celery, and stock, along with a large pinch of salt, if using unsalted stock. Bring to a boil, reduce the heat, cover, and cook gently for about 20 minutes, until the vegetables are tender.

Allow the soup to cool slightly, then transfer to a food processor or blender, working in batches if necessary. Purée the soup until smooth. (If using a food processor, strain off the cooking liquid and reserve it. Purée the soup solids with enough cooking liquid to moisten them, then combine with the remaining liquid.)

Transfer the puréed soup into a large container. Cover and refrigerate until cold.

Stir the cream, salmon, and chives into the soup. If time permits, chill for at least 1 hour to allow the flavors to blend. Taste and adjust the seasoning, adding salt, if needed, and pepper. Ladle into chilled bowls and serve.

4

Spicy Soups

This chapter explores the world of spice, with an exciting selection of internationally inspired dishes. The recipes range in heat from the warming Mushroom & Ginger Soup to the carefully balanced Hot & Sour Soup with Tofu, and from the fiery Pork Chili Soup to the delicately spiced Thai Chicken-Coconut Soup. All are guaranteed to spice up and add excitement to your meals.

Hot & Sour Soup with Tofu

Put the lime rind, garlic, and ginger into a large pan with the stock and bring to a boil. Reduce the heat and let simmer for 5 minutes. Remove the lime rind, garlic, and ginger with a slotted spoon and discard.

Meanwhile, heat the vegetable oil in a large skillet over high heat, add the tofu, and cook, turning frequently, until golden. Remove from the skillet and drain on paper towels.

Add the noodles, mushrooms, and chile to the stock and let simmer for 3 minutes.

Add the tofu, scallions, soy sauce, lime juice, rice wine, and sesame oil and briefly heat through.

Divide the soup among 4 warmed bowls, sprinkle over the cilantro, and serve at once.

SERVES 4

3 strips of rind and juice of 1 lime
2 garlic cloves, peeled
2 slices fresh ginger
4 cups chicken stock
1 tbsp vegetable oil
5 1/2 oz/150 g firm tofu (drained weight), cubed
7 oz/200 g dried fine egg noodles
3 1/2 oz/100 g shiitake mushrooms, sliced
1 fresh red chile, seeded and sliced
4 scallions, sliced
1 tsp soy sauce
1 tsp Chinese rice wine
1 tsp sesame oil
chopped fresh cilantro, to garnish

Mushroom & Ginger Soup

Soak the dried Chinese mushrooms for at least 30 minutes in 1¼ cups of the hot stock. Drain the mushrooms and reserve the stock. Remove the stems of the mushrooms and discard. Slice the caps and reserve. Cook the noodles for 2–3 minutes in boiling water, then drain and rinse. Reserve until required.

Heat the corn oil in a preheated wok or large, heavy-bottom skillet over high heat. Add the garlic and ginger, stir, and add the mushrooms. Stir over high heat for 2 minutes.

Add the remaining vegetable stock with the reserved mushroom stock and bring to a boil. Add the soy sauce. Stir in the bean sprouts and cook until tender.

Place some noodles in each soup bowl and ladle the soup on top. Garnish with fresh cilantro sprigs and serve immediately.

SERVES 4

- 1/2 oz/15 g dried Chinese mushrooms or 4 1/2 oz/125 g portobello or cremini mushrooms
- 4 cups hot vegetable stock
- 4 1/2 oz/125 g thin egg noodles
- 2 tsp corn oil
- 3 garlic cloves, crushed
- 1-inch/2.5-cm piece fresh ginger, finely shredded
- 1 tsp light soy sauce
- 4 1/2 oz/125 g bean sprouts
- fresh cilantro sprigs, to garnish

Thai Chicken-Coconut Soup

SERVES 4

4 oz/115 g dried cellophane noodles
5 cups chicken or vegetable stock
1 lemongrass stalk, crushed
1/2-inch/1-cm piece fresh ginger, peeled and very finely chopped
2 fresh kaffir lime leaves, thinly sliced
1 fresh red chile, or to taste, seeded and thinly sliced
2 skinless, boneless chicken breasts, thinly sliced
1 cup coconut cream
2 tbsp nam pla (Thai fish sauce)
1 tbsp fresh lime juice
1/2 cup bean sprouts
4 scallions, green part only, finely sliced
fresh cilantro leaves, to garnish

Soak the dried noodles in a large bowl with enough lukewarm water to cover for 20 minutes, until soft. Alternatively, cook according to the package instructions. Drain well and set aside.

Meanwhile, bring the stock to a boil in a large pan over high heat. Lower the heat, add the lemongrass, ginger, lime leaves, and chile and simmer for 5 minutes. Add the chicken and continue simmering for an additional 3 minutes, or until cooked. Stir in the coconut cream, nam pla, and lime juice and continue simmering for 3 minutes. Add the bean sprouts and scallions and simmer for an additional 1 minute. Taste and gradually add extra nam pla or lime juice at this point, if needed. Remove and discard the lemongrass stalk.

Divide the noodles among 4 bowls. Bring the soup back to a boil, then ladle into the bowls. The heat of the soup will warm the noodles. To garnish, sprinkle with cilantro leaves.

Duck with Scallion Soup

Slash the skin of the duck 3 or 4 times with a sharp knife and rub in the curry paste. Cook the duck breasts, skin-side down, in a wok or skillet over high heat for 2–3 minutes. Turn over, reduce the heat, and cook for an additional 3–4 minutes, until cooked through. Lift out and slice thickly. Set aside and keep warm.

Meanwhile, heat the oil in a wok or large skillet and stir-fry half the scallions, the garlic, ginger, carrots, and red bell pepper for 2–3 minutes. Pour in the stock and add the chili sauce, soy sauce, and mushrooms. Bring to a boil, reduce the heat, and simmer for 4–5 minutes.

Ladle the soup into warmed bowls, top with the duck slices, and garnish with the remaining scallions. Serve immediately.

SERVES 4

2 duck breasts, skin on
2 tbsp red curry paste
2 tbsp vegetable or peanut oil
bunch of scallions, chopped
2 garlic cloves, crushed
2-inch/5-cm piece fresh ginger, grated
2 carrots, thinly sliced
1 red bell pepper, seeded and cut into strips
4 cups chicken stock
2 tbsp sweet chili sauce
3–4 tbsp Thai soy sauce
14 oz/400 g canned straw mushrooms, drained

Pork Chili Soup

SERVES 4

2 tsp olive oil
1 lb 2 oz/500 g fresh lean ground pork
1 onion, finely chopped
1 celery stalk, finely chopped
1 red bell pepper, cored, seeded, and finely chopped
2–3 garlic cloves, finely chopped
3 tbsp tomato paste
14 oz/400 g canned chopped tomatoes
2 cups chicken or meat stock
1/8 tsp ground coriander
1/8 tsp ground cumin
1/4 tsp dried oregano
1 tsp mild chili powder, or to taste
salt and pepper
fresh cilantro leaves, to garnish
sour cream, to serve

Heat the oil in a large, saucepan over medium-high heat. Add the pork, season with salt and pepper, and cook until no longer pink, stirring frequently. Reduce the heat to medium and add the onion, celery, red bell pepper, and garlic. Cover and continue cooking for 5 minutes, stirring occasionally, until the onion is softened.

Add the tomato paste, tomatoes, and the stock. Add the coriander, cumin, oregano, and chili powder. Stir the ingredients in to combine well.

Bring just to a boil, reduce the heat to low, cover, and simmer for 30–40 minutes, until all the vegetables are very tender. Taste and adjust the seasoning, adding more chili powder if you like it hotter.

Ladle the chili into warmed bowls and sprinkle with cilantro. Top each serving with a spoonful of sour cream and serve.

Corn, Chile & Chorizo Soup

Heat the oil in a large heavy-bottom pan. Add the onions and cook over low heat, stirring occasionally, for 5 minutes, or until softened. Stir in the corn, cover, and cook for an additional 3 minutes.

Add the stock, half the milk, the chiles, and garlic and season with salt. Bring to a boil, reduce the heat, then cover and simmer for 15–20 minutes.

Stir in the remaining milk. Set aside about 3/4 cup of the soup solids, draining off as much liquid as possible. Transfer the remaining soup to a food processor or blender and process to a coarse purée.

Return the soup to the pan and stir in the reserved soup solids, the chorizo, lime juice, and cilantro. Reheat to the simmering point, stirring constantly. Ladle into warmed bowls and serve at once.

SERVES 4

1 tbsp corn oil
2 onions, chopped
1 lb 4 oz/550 g frozen corn kernels, thawed
2 1/2 cups chicken stock
2 cups milk
4 chipotle chiles, seeded and finely chopped
2 garlic cloves, finely chopped
2 oz/55 g thinly sliced chorizo sausage
2 tbsp lime juice
2 tbsp chopped fresh cilantro
salt

Spicy Beef & Noodle Soup

Pour the stock into a large pan and bring to a boil. Meanwhile, heat the oil in a wok or large skillet. Add one-third of the noodles and cook for 10–20 seconds, until they have puffed up. Lift out with tongs, drain on paper towels, and set aside. Discard all but 2 tablespoons of the oil.

Add the shallots, garlic, and ginger to the wok or skillet and stir-fry for 1 minute. Add the beef and curry paste and stir-fry for an additional 3–4 minutes, until tender.

Add the beef mixture, the uncooked noodles, soy sauce, and fish sauce to the pan of stock and simmer for 2–3 minutes, until the noodles have swelled. Serve hot, garnished with the chopped cilantro and the reserved crispy noodles.

SERVES 4

4 cups beef stock
2/3 cup vegetable or peanut oil
3 oz/85 g rice vermicelli noodles
2 shallots, sliced thinly
2 garlic cloves, crushed
1-inch/2.5-cm piece fresh ginger, sliced thinly
8-oz/225-g piece beef tenderloin, cut into thin strips
2 tbsp Thai green curry paste
2 tbsp Thai soy sauce
1 tbsp fish sauce
chopped fresh cilantro, to garnish

Asian Lamb Soup

Trim all visible fat from the lamb and slice the meat thinly. Cut the slices into bite-sized pieces. Spread the meat in one layer on a plate and sprinkle over the garlic and 1 tablespoon of the soy sauce. Let marinate, covered, for at least 10 minutes or up to 1 hour.

Put the stock in a saucepan with the ginger, lemongrass, remaining soy sauce, and the chili paste. Bring just to a boil, reduce the heat, cover, and simmer for 10–15 minutes.

When ready to serve the soup, drop the tomatoes, scallions, bean sprouts, and cilantro leaves into the stock.

Heat the oil in a skillet and add the lamb with its marinade. Stir-fry the lamb just until it is no longer red and divide among the warmed bowls.

Ladle over the hot stock and serve immediately.

SERVES 4

- 5 1/2 oz/150 g lean tender lamb, such as neck fillet or leg steak
- 2 garlic cloves, very finely chopped
- 2 tbsp soy sauce
- 5 cups chicken stock
- 1 tbsp grated fresh ginger
- 2-inch/5-cm piece lemongrass, sliced into very thin rounds
- 1/4 tsp chili paste, or to taste
- 6–8 cherry tomatoes, quartered
- 4 scallions, sliced finely
- 1 3/4 oz/50 g bean sprouts, snapped in half
- 2 tbsp cilantro leaves
- 1 tsp olive oil

Corn & Crab Soup

SERVES 6

- 2 tbsp vegetable or peanut oil
- 4 garlic cloves, finely chopped
- 5 shallots, finely chopped
- 2 lemongrass stalks, finely chopped
- 1-inch/2.5-cm piece fresh ginger, finely chopped
- 4 cups chicken stock
- 14 oz/400 g canned coconut milk
- $1^1/_2$ cups frozen corn kernels
- 12 oz/350 g canned crabmeat, drained and shredded
- 2 tbsp fish sauce
- juice of 1 lime
- 1 tsp jaggery or light brown sugar
- bunch of fresh cilantro, chopped, to garnish

Heat the oil in a large skillet and sauté the garlic, shallots, lemongrass, and ginger over low heat, stirring occasionally, for 2–3 minutes, until softened. Add the stock and coconut milk and bring to a boil. Add the corn, reduce the heat, and simmer gently for 3–4 minutes.

Add the crabmeat, fish sauce, lime juice, and sugar, and simmer gently for 1 minute. Ladle into warmed bowls, garnish with the chopped cilantro, and serve immediately.

Thai-Style Seafood Soup

Put the stock in a saucepan with the lemongrass, lime rind, ginger, and chili paste. Bring just to a boil, reduce the heat, cover, and simmer for 10–15 minutes.

Cut the shrimp almost in half lengthwise, keeping the tail intact.

Strain the stock, return to the saucepan, and bring to a simmer. Add the scallions and cook for 2–3 minutes. Taste and season with salt, if needed, and stir in a little more chili paste if desired.

Add the scallops and shrimp and poach for about 1 minute, until they turn opaque and the shrimp curl.

Stir in the fresh cilantro leaves, ladle the soup into warmed bowls, dividing the shellfish evenly, and garnish with chiles.

SERVES 4

5 cups fish stock
1 lemongrass stalk, split lengthwise
pared rind of 1/2 lime, or 1 lime leaf
1-inch/2.5-cm piece fresh ginger, sliced
1/4 tsp chili paste, or to taste
7 oz/200 g large or medium raw shrimp, peeled
4–6 scallions, sliced
9 oz/250 g scallops
2 tbsp fresh cilantro leaves
salt
finely sliced red chiles, to garnish